Ultimate Affiliate Marketing with Blogging Quick Start Guide

KIP PIPER

http://www.kippiperbooks.com

Copyright © 2013 by Kip Piper

All Rights Reserved

ISBN: 1-886522-10-3
ISBN-13: 978-1-886522-10-7

YOUR FREE GIFT…

Want a free book? Want access to more freebies and special offers through Amazon?

As a way of saying *thanks* for your purchase, I'm offering a free eBook that is only available to my customers. Right now, you can get a copy of my book: *"28-Day Small Business Profit Plan: The Quick Start Guide for Business Success"*. This book is not sold anywhere else and can only be found on my website.

Plus, you will learn how to get instant notification whenever there is a **new free book** or **special book bundles** through Amazon.

Get the details at my website: **www.KipPiperBooks.com**

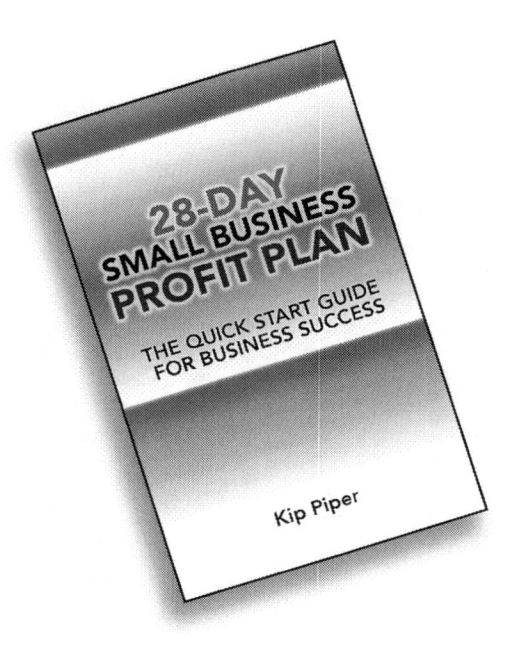

CONTENTS

Author's Note i
A Few Words From Kip 1
3 Top Reasons for Not Blogging 5
Who is Kip Piper? 6
How I Started Blogging 9
Built My First Blog Affiliate Marketing Website 10
Does Blog Affiliate Marketing Work? 12
What We Will Cover 13
Research & Choose Your Niche 14
Find Sources of Income 26
Build Your Blog Website 30
Your Domain – Your Company Name 32
Develop Content 35
Incorporating Income Links 38
Ranking in Google 41
"Wash, Rinse, Repeat" 43
One Last Thing… 45
Resources 46
In Their Own Words 47
About the Author 51
More Books by Kip Piper 52
Become a Part of the Make Money Online Entrepreneur Series ... 55

AUTHOR'S NOTE

As you have probably experienced, the Internet and the websites on it are constantly changing. The information, examples, and screenshots presented in this book are accurate at the time of publication.

If you encounter any websites that have changed, please let me know by emailing me at: kip@kippiperbooks.com.

Remember, even though the website(s) may have changed, the principles, techniques and strategies in this book remain sound.

For your convenience, all websites, tools, and software mentioned in this book are listed in the RESOURCES section at the end of this book.

The links provided are primarily affiliate links, which means if you purchase through the links, I receive a commission. This is the heart of affiliate marketing and entrepreneurship – which I am teaching you how to do with this book! I thank you in advance for using the affiliate links.

A FEW WORDS FROM KIP

Before I began teaching others how to blog and be successful with their online businesses, I wanted to be sure that I had something different to teach – strategies that are not easily found but can make a huge impact on success. The last thing I wanted to do is waste anyone's time. I wanted to offer something unique that would add both value and the potential for quick success for you.

Unknowingly, my research into online business success began in 1996 when I was first introduced to the concept of affiliate marketing. The potential for income excited me and I was quick to start experimenting with it. I joined Amazon.com and the few other affiliate programs available at the time. I added links on my website to products that related to my web design and Internet marketing business, with the purpose of offering quality resources to my website visitors and my clients. I encouraged and worked with my clients to include affiliate marketing in their overall online presence. I did this all in the hopes of adding to my income streams and eventually have affiliate marketing my dominant, if not sole, source of income.

But it did not come quickly, as others had promised or experienced. I totally, 100% believed in the concept of an online business and affiliate marketing (and still do), I understood the mechanics of setting up websites, creating products, and adding affiliate links, but I struggled with ranking my site high with the search engines and driving traffic to my site. Where were all the promised visitors who would buy what I offered or recommended so I could earn commissions?

Why were so many others achieving success? Why wasn't I experiencing the same success? Where was I going wrong?

I joined various mastermind groups. I purchased training programs from so-called "gurus". I bought books, read articles, watched videos, attended conference calls and webinars – I immersed myself in learning about blogging, affiliate marketing, and creating products.

The one most important thing I learned is that you need multiple websites, each focused on a different niche, to ensure a steady stream of income. "But," I asked, "if I can't get people to come to my first website, why should I spend more money and time creating websites that will not be visited either?" And each "guru" smiled nicely and said, "If you will upgrade your membership to our most expensive level, I'll tell you." But when I looked closely, I realized each "guru" was not living the life I wanted. In fact, most were working as hard or harder than I – with even less free time and income! They did not have the freedom of time and money that I wanted.

I didn't give up, though. I continued my search – knowing the one little "missing link" was out there.

One day I found it!

With this new knowledge, I knew without a doubt I could not only be personally successful with blogging, affiliate marketing and product creation, but now I could teach others those same strategies.

I realized that knowledge is what sets apart the training I offer – with this book and my other books which you can find at **http://www.kippiperbooks.com**.

This book is unique because it was written for *YOU*.

- YOU are someone who sees the potential in having an online business of affiliate marketing and product creation, but needs to know how to get started.
- YOU want practical strategies and advice that have already been tested and proven to work.
- YOU are ready for double-digit growth in sales.
- YOU are committed to following through with what you're about to learn.

This is why YOU are here.

Now please understand. Every piece of advice, strategy and practice has been tested on actual live blog, affiliate marketing and product websites – my own, my clients', and others. None of this is theory. You might then ask yourself, *ok, so how many blogs and affiliate websites has Kip done and what qualifies her as an "internet business expert"?* I think that's a great question. I wish more people questioned so called "experts" to see what qualifies them. As for me, I looked back on the last 15 years of stats and discovered that I have personally generated a 5-figure income in blogging, affiliate marketing and my own product sales – and that's just part-time!

If that's something you'd like to accomplish, you've selected the right book and series to begin with. I say "begin" because you'll soon discover that the learning process is a journey.

But don't worry! There's one more thing that qualifies me to lead you down this path – I'm just like you. It doesn't matter if you've never built a website or if you're already earning an income with blogging, affiliate marketing and your own product, and simply want to improve your sales. As you have already read, I've been wherever you are right now.

For anyone who reads this book and the entire *"Make Money Online Entrepreneur Series"*, and implements everything they learn, I can guarantee your business will move forward with more subscribers, sales and a stronger connection to your market. Like I said before, it doesn't matter if you've never built a website in your life or if you're already experienced, I've been there and can show you how to make blogging, affiliate marketing and product creation a successful income source.

But before we begin, I need you to do something. Connect with me on Facebook at:

http://www.facebook.com/TheRandomBlondeFanPage

I'd love to stay in touch and learn more about your journey.

You also are invited to check my website for more business books, and all of the books included in this *"Making Money Online Entrepreneur Series"*:

http://www.kippiperbooks.com

Thanks again for choosing to spend this time with me. Now let's get started!

"Done is better than Perfect!"

3 TOP REASONS FOR NOT BLOGGING

I have found three top reasons why people don't blog. They are:

- **I don't know how.** Some of you are scared of the technology. Some of you are just not sure what it all means.
- **I can't write.** Some of you say "I can't write" so you're not going to even try to write new articles or blog posts. You're embarrassed about your writing.
- **It's too much work!** And some of you say just way too much work.

Well, the first two we're going cover today in this book.

The last one – too much work – well, I don't agree. If you really want to make a serious income from blogging, obviously you have to work on it consistently but you can start with just 2 to 5 hours a week for a nice, steady income. So you don't have to invest a lot of time to make it successful.

WHO IS KIP PIPER?

A little bit about me. Some of you already know me, some of you don't!

I've been a web designer and Internet marketer since 1993. Yup! Almost 20 years! It just totally changed my business. This was back with my late husband, and we just had a ball adding websites to the corporate marketing package that we offered to our customers. In addition to standard business cards, brochures and things like that, we added websites.

Over the years, I have built websites and provided the Internet marketing for several hundred customers – from entrepreneurs and small businesses to Fortune 100 companies, including:

3M
DELL
AMD
THE UNIVERSITY OF TEXAS AT AUSTIN
HYUNDAI STEEL USA

I've been a blog designer, and blog and social media marketer, since 2009. I've been a trainer in all sorts of different area since 1978.

I love putting together training programs. I love teaching people and I love teaching systems – which is why this book is perfect because I'm going to show you a system for blogging and affiliate marketing.

To give you a little bit of background of where I've come from, I've worked in private industry; I've been a federal government employee; and I've been self employed for over 20 years.

So I do understand how many of you may feel about the current economy and having to depend on someone else for your income. My goal is to show you a solution that you can start using right away to create extra income and eventually turn it into full time income.

HOW I STARTED BLOGGING

So, you may be asking how did I get into blogging.

Back in 2008, I was invited to stay at a friend's house in San Angelo, Texas, and house sit for them. They had put the house in the market, and had moved into their next house.

This house is huge! It's 5000 square feet and has 4 bedrooms, 2.5 baths, plus a 2-bedroom apartment, plus a 1-bedroom apartment, plus an attached 3-car garage, and a detached 2- car garage, and 2 outbuildings, and a swimming pool, and just much more than I could possibly list here. I was very blessed to be able to live in this house being the house sitter. I had a chance to learn about the house and see how it was to live in it.

My friends, the owners, had a real estate agent for 1 full year, which is a standard contract for real estate agents. During that time, the agent did not bring one, single, qualified potential buyer to the house. They showed it maybe, *maybe* 10-12 times. They did not take the time to learn the features of this house – and there were tons of them. This house is very unique, obviously. It had many wonderful features that were built in – features you don't find typically in today's homes.

After the owners fired the real estate agent, they tried "for sale by owner". After about a month of not even a nibble, I said to them, "Let me build you a website" to get the word out about this house. I had been hearing about blogs and how powerful they were for marketing and selling products and services. That is why I recommended a blog website. They said "Yes!", and this was my first foray into the blogging world – and jumping right in to using the blog to sell a product.

BUILT MY FIRST BLOG AFFILIATE MARKETING WEBSITE

To see what I did, the website address for the house is:

http://sanangelohouseforsale.Wordpress.com

I started the blog website on March 2, 2009, which was a Sunday. By Thursday, March 6, the blog website ranked on the first page of Google – above almost all of the other San Angelo and national real estate websites, including Coldwell-Banker, ReMax, MLS – it just jumped right to the top. Over the next months, the house was shown several times to people who inquired from the website. In early November of that year, we showed the house once again, and on November 24, the people made an offer. The offer was accepted, and on December 29 the sale closed.

So in nine months from the time that I put up this blog website, the house was sold. Now something to remember – this was right after the housing market crashed. This was a $500,000+ home. So it was hard to sell a home like this in that market, not to mention the fact that this is a very unique house that required a family who could take advantage of all it had to offer. Obviously, the owners were thrilled.

Just out of curiosity [as I am writing this on November 12, 2012], I went on to the internet and I put in "San Angelo house for sale" in quotes in Google, and this website *still* ranks on the first page of Google – as Number 3! I have not posted to this website in three years. If you do the same thing and search on Google for "San Angelo" + "house for sale" or "house for sale in San Angelo", either the website shows up or links to YouTube videos about the house.

ULTIMATE AFFILIATE MARKETING WITH BLOGGING QUICK START GUIDE

Google "san angelo house for sale"

Web   Images   Maps   Shopping   More ▾   Search tools

About 5,110 results (0.32 seconds)

San Angelo House For Sale - WordPress.com — Get a Free Blog H...
en.wordpress.com/tag/san-angelo-house-for-sale/
SOLD!!! We are very excited to announce that this house has SOLD! We also want to say that, of all the people who viewed the house, only the truly qualified ...

San Angelo House for sale - Yellowpages.com
www.yellowpages.com/san-angelo/house-for-sale
Results 1 - 30 of 112 – 112 listings of Real Estate Agents in San Angelo on YP.com. Find reviews, directions & phone numbers for the best house for sale in San ...

Beautiful Spacious House for Sale in San Angelo, Texas
sanangelohouseforsale.wordpress.com/
Enjoy Legendary West Texas Lifestyle in the Prestigious Butler Farms Estates of San Angelo (by BA)

San Angelo house for sale by owner - San Angelo Classifieds - Kijiji
sanangelo.ebayclassifieds.com/classified-ads/?q=house...
20+ items – Find **San Angelo house for sale** by owner dogs & puppies, cats ...
$600   **Miniature/Toy Australian Shepherds** 4 Blue Merle ...
Please contact for price   2 Guinea pigs + cage + accesories

San Angelo house for sale | Dogs | TVs | Jobs | eBay Classifieds ...
sanangelo.ebayclassifieds.com/classified-ads/?q=house+for...
Find **San Angelo house for sale** dogs & puppies, cats & kittens, electronics, DVDs, TVs, and Jobs. Best free local ads from eBay Classifieds - Page 1.

DOES BLOG AFFILIATE MARKETING WORK?

So you can see, blog affiliate marketing works! It works for marketing and selling a product. The owner/seller of the house says, "The only qualified prospects came from the website including the buyer. I would not have sold the house so soon and at such a good price without the blog website."

This sold me on blogging to market a product. It convinced me that this is a very powerful way to market a product, market it to a targeted audience, and get it noticed fast.

How did I do this?

Well that's what we're going to cover in this book.

WHAT WE WILL COVER

So what we're going to cover in this book is:

- How to research and choose your niche
- How to find sources of income
- How to build your blog website
- How to develop content
- How to incorporate income links
- The secrets to ranking in Google
- "Wash, Rinse, and Repeat"

RESEARCH & CHOOSE YOUR NICHE

The first step is to research and choose your niche. It is best to start with a niche that you are passionate about, or at least knowledgeable.

There are some great free tools and also some great paid tools out there to help you with your market research. Proper market research will help make sure there are enough people interested in your niche to read your blog and purchase the products you recommend. Without a large targeted audience, your chances of income become more difficult.

Google Trends

So, one great place is Google Trends http://www.google.com/trends/. This free tool shows the most popular searches; it shows activity over time; it shows countries and cities of searches; and keyword variations.

ULTIMATE AFFILIATE MARKETING WITH BLOGGING QUICK START GUIDE

Above is a screenshot of the opening page of Google Trends. On this page you have a field where you can type in the niche terms that you're looking for. Below that field, you can see the examples of the format they suggest. One important thing is to use multiple word terms – the more words you use (to a point), the more targeted your results.

Say you want to have a travel blogging website. If you just type in "travel", you're going to be competing with millions of other websites. But if you type in "vacation travel in Costa Rica", then you're going to have much fewer sites to compete with.

Further down this front page of Google Trends, you'll see the hot searches of the last few days, which gives you an idea what the trends are currently. **Do *not*** fall victim to going after current trends. The public is fickle, and by the time you get a website built, that trend has come and gone.

So, for example, let's conduct a trends research on "baby clothes". Once you type in "baby clothes" in the field and hit "Explore", you are taken to the next page.

This next page shows the search trends for the keyword phrase "baby clothes". [See next screenshot.] When you look closely, the graph shows the search trends for "baby clothes" since 2004. The graph also shows you what time of the year the searches have been at the highest and the lowest.

As you can see, this is a great example of an "evergreen" market in that "baby clothes" has a consistent number of searches every month, every year.

Interest over time
The number 100 represents the peak search interest

☑ News headlines   ☐ Forecast

Regional interest

Related terms   Top | Rising

baby girl clothes	100
baby boy clothes	95
baby clothing	95
baby clothes online	70
kids clothes	65
newborn clothes	55
newborn baby	55
newborn baby clothes	55
cheap baby clothes	55
gap baby clothes	50

The page also shows you related search terms below the graph. If you hover your mouse over different dates of the trends graph, you can see what was popular on those particular dates. It gives you all of the related searches around "baby clothes" – both those that apply to your area of interest and those that don't.

You can also see the countries and the quantity of searches; and with the United States, you see the cities with the highest number of searches.

So Google Trends is one of the ways you can research how a often a search term/keyword phrase for you niche is actually searched. Then ask yourself, is it a powerful niche? Are people searching on it, and if so, when?

Google Keyword Planner

The other free tool is the Google Keyword Planner https://adwords.google.com/ko/KeywordPlanner.

Google Keyword Planner is part of Google Adwords. You *MUST* have an account with Google Adwords to use the Google Keyword Planner. But not to worry! Creating a Google Adwords account is free.

Once you're logged in to Google AdWords, you can find the Keyword Planner by looking under the Tools an Analysis menu. Once you're there, you have three options. For determining the strength of a market and niche, you want to select "Search for keyword and ad group ideas:

| Home | Campaigns | Opportunities | Tools and Analysis ▾ | Billing |

Keyword Planner
Plan your next search campaign

What would you like to do?

▸ Search for keyword and ad group ideas

▸ Enter or upload keywords to see how they perform

▸ Multiply keyword lists

So, in the screenshot below, you will see the "Search for keyword and ad group ideas" field at the top where we can type in "baby clothes". Then click on "Get ideas".

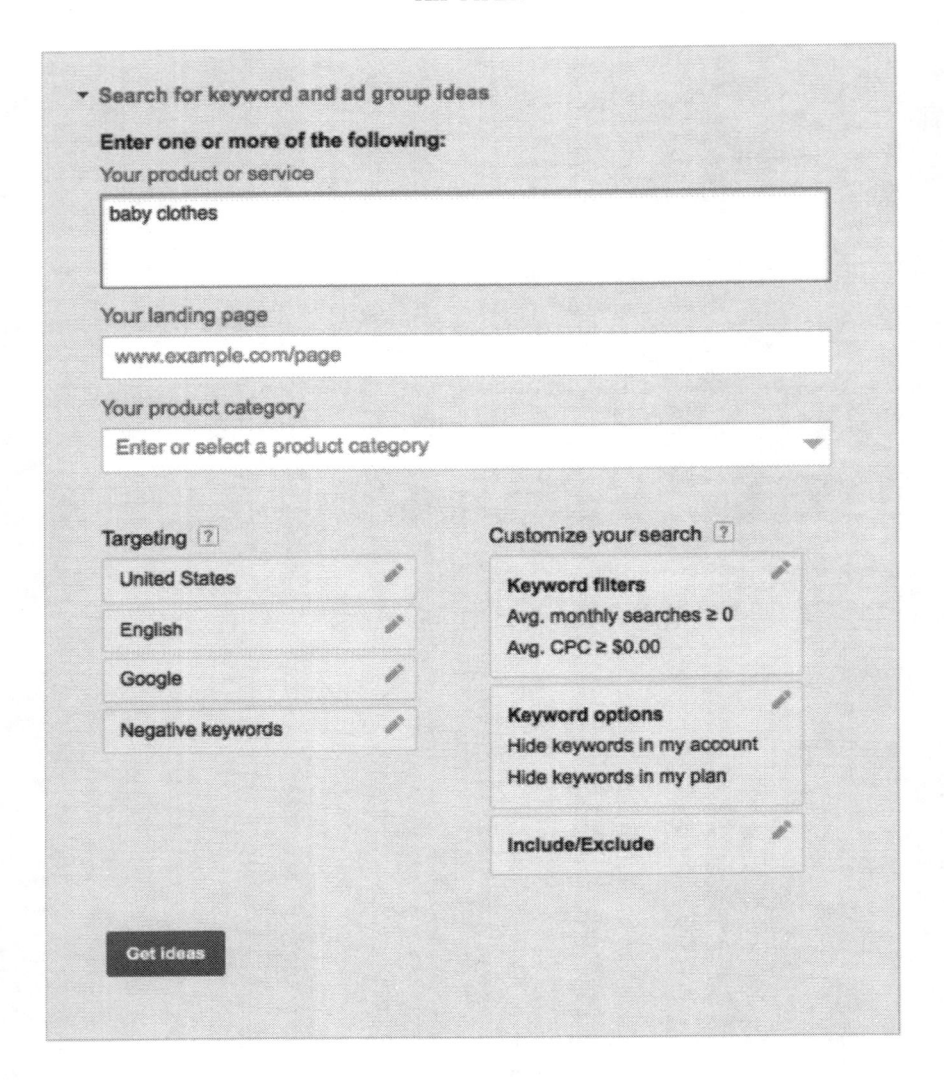

On the next screen, click on the "Keyword ideas" tab. The screenshot below shows the results from "baby clothes". The results for the exact phrase "baby clothes" appear on the top line. It shows to have 74,000 global searches and the competition is "high". Then further down you will see the related phrases and their results.

Search terms	Avg. monthly searches	Competition	Avg. CPC	
baby clothes	74,000	High	$1.59	»

1 - 1 of 1 keywords

Keyword (by relevance)	Avg. monthly searches	Competition	Avg. CPC	
baby names	823,000	Low	$0.29	»
carters	450,000	Low	$0.09	»
maternity clothes	201,000	High	$1.15	»
baby	165,000	Low	$1.25	»
baby depot	49,500	Low	$0.08	»
free baby stuff	33,100	High	$0.98	»
baby shoes	27,100	High	$0.84	»
kids clothes	27,100	High	$1.23	»
baby boy clothes	22,200	High	$0.82	»
baby girl clothes	22,200	High	$0.92	»
baby stores	22,200	High	$0.85	»

Google Keyword Planner is great place to get ideas on the types of keyword phrases you can use to market and find your target audience. What you want at least 3,000 searches a month, and "Low" competition under the "Competition" column. "Competition" means how many other websites are using that exact keyword phrase somewhere in their site – either their domain name, title of the site, headline on the home page, and keywords on the home page. The lower the competition, the better you'll have a chance of beating them in the search engines. So that's an important part of this market research.

With Google Keyword Planner, you will find out first if people are actually searching on the niche that you're interested in promoting. If so, then you need to see if the niche is getting enough searches and is the competition low enough to make it worth your while to build a website and market to this audience. That's part of your market research.

However, the downside of Google Keyword Tool is its use of the competition terms "Low", "Medium", and "High". These terms are subjective and open to broad interpretation – none of it guaranteed to be accurate.

Paid Keyword Research Tools

Instead, wouldn't it be great to know *exactly* how many other websites are in competition with you for your keyword phrases? Of course! So that leads us to our next market research tool.

Niche Builder **http://kippiperbooks.com/NicheBuilder** is a paid tool. The first tools, Google Trends and Google Keyword Planner, are free. As a paid tool, Niche Builder is very powerful. You can start with it now or you can wait until a little bit later. It all depends on how you want to approach developing your website for your niche. What Niche Builder does is give you much more power in being able to precisely know and target your prospective audience in REAL TIME, therefore realizing income even faster.

The screenshot below is the front page of the website. It explains about Niche Builder, which has incredible training modules for every aspect of using this very sophisticated tool. You can try it and see how you like it – it comes with a money back guarantee!

ULTIMATE AFFILIATE MARKETING WITH BLOGGING QUICK START GUIDE

The next screenshot shows the opening dashboard of Niche Builder. It is a very powerful tool and is built on a huge database. It provides the most current, up-to-date, real time information I have found so far. This makes it a very valuable tool because it gives you so much more information than either Google Trends or Google Keyword Planner.

You research your niche by entering your keyword phrase. *(NOTE: I am not going to give step by step instructions here, because Niche Builder's training is much better!)* Niche Builder will not only bring back the number of searches in the last 30 days, but most important, the actual number of websites that use that same keyword phrase in their website.

Once you have your raw results from Niche Builder, you want to select those related keyword phrases that met two criteria:

- Prospective keywords that have at least 3,000 searches a month
- Competition of less than 300,000 other websites.

So staying with our "baby clothes" niche research, I did a keyword search for "baby clothes". And the results of the keyword search resulted in 136 possible related keyword phrases, as you can see in the next screenshot.

ULTIMATE AFFILIATE MARKETING WITH BLOGGING QUICK START GUIDE

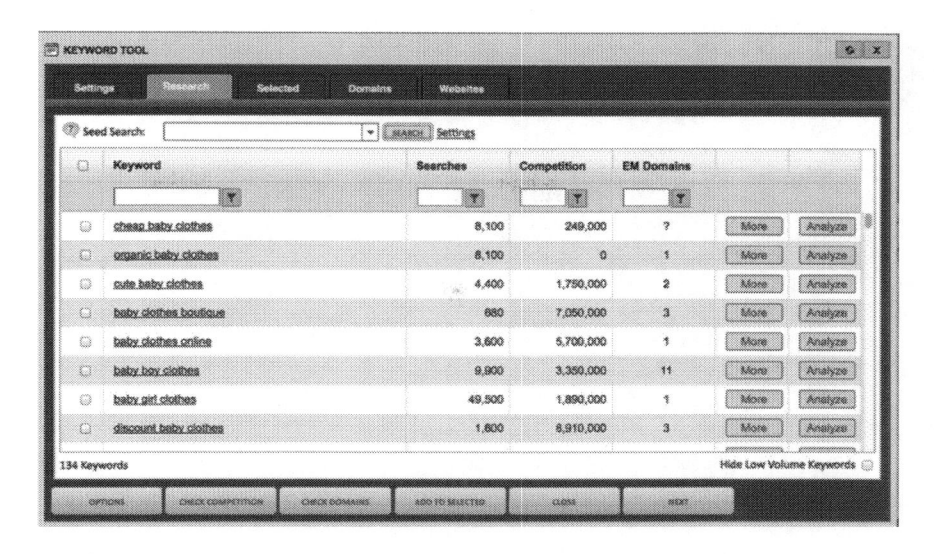

Keyword	Searches	Competition	EM Domains
cheap baby clothes	8,100	249,000	?
organic baby clothes	8,100	0	1
cute baby clothes	4,400	1,750,000	2
baby clothes boutique	880	7,050,000	3
baby clothes online	3,600	5,700,000	1
baby boy clothes	9,900	3,350,000	11
baby girl clothes	49,500	1,890,000	1
discount baby clothes	1,800	6,910,000	3

134 Keywords

Next, I narrowed them down to the 10 keyword phrases that have at least 3,000 people who search "baby clothes" each month and have less than 400,000 competition. (I made the judgment call to allow a little more than 300,000 competition to increase my options. **See my "Important Note" below**.) Here are the results:

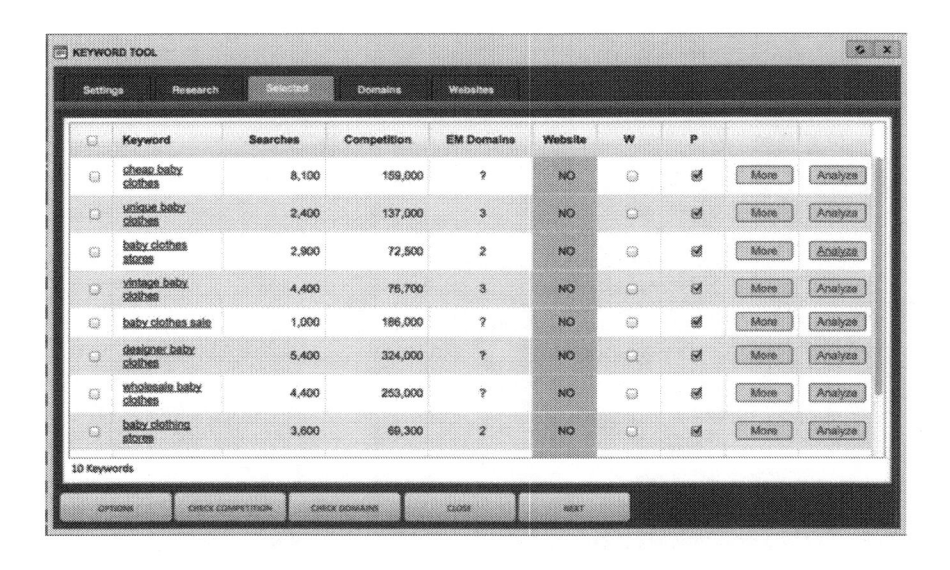

Keyword	Searches	Competition	EM Domains	Website	W	P
cheap baby clothes	8,100	159,000	?	NO		✓
unique baby clothes	2,400	137,000	3	NO		✓
baby clothes stores	2,900	72,500	2	NO		✓
vintage baby clothes	4,400	76,700	3	NO		✓
baby clothes sale	1,000	186,000	?	NO		✓
designer baby clothes	5,400	324,000	?	NO		✓
wholesale baby clothes	4,400	253,000	?	NO		✓
baby clothing stores	3,600	69,300	2	NO		✓

10 Keywords

23

Niche Builder also gives you ability to analyze each one of these keyword phrases. When you click on the "Analyze" button next to a keyword phrase, you see a chart of the top ten Google search results for that phrase. In the next screenshot, I chose to analyze the phrase "cheap baby clothes".

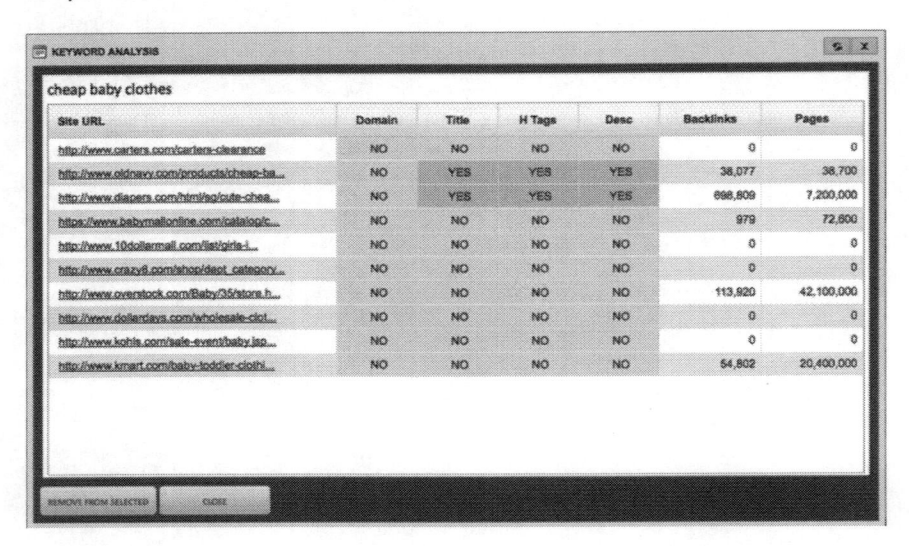

Site URL	Domain	Title	H Tags	Desc	Backlinks	Pages
http://www.carters.com/carters-clearance	NO	NO	NO	NO	0	0
http://www.oldnavy.com/products/cheap-ba...	NO	YES	YES	YES	38,077	38,700
http://www.diapers.com/html/ag/cute-chea...	NO	YES	YES	YES	698,809	7,200,000
https://www.babymallonline.com/catalog/c...	NO	NO	NO	NO	979	72,600
http://www.10dollarmall.com/list/girls-i...	NO	NO	NO	NO	0	0
http://www.crazy8.com/shop/dept_category...	NO	NO	NO	NO	0	0
http://www.overstock.com/Baby/35/store.h...	NO	NO	NO	NO	113,920	42,100,000
http://www.dollardays.com/wholesale-clot...	NO	NO	NO	NO	0	0
http://www.kohls.com/sale-event/baby.jsp...	NO	NO	NO	NO	0	0
http://www.kmart.com/baby-toddler-clothi...	NO	NO	NO	NO	54,802	20,400,000

The resulting chart tells you a number of things, such as:

- Does that website have "cheap baby clothes" in their domain name? No.
- Is it in their website title? No.
- Is it in their headline tags? No.
- Is it in their website description? No.

This all means that, if you have the words "cheap baby clothes" in your domain, in your title, in your headline tags, and in your website description, you can beat them out. You can really make to the first page in Google! It is simple as that. Yes, it does take work, but it's as simple as that. As you can see in this chart, most of the websites do NOT have the keyword phrase "cheap baby clothes" in any of the critical website elements. And the two that do, do not have it in the domain name. These sites are not fully optimized for this keyword phrase.

As you can see, there is significant value to this tool. As I mentioned earlier, it is a monthly subscription, comes with the money back guarantee, and you can cancel it at any time.

I guarantee you it is well worth the investment – if only for your time!

Let me give you a real-life example:

Before I had access to this tool (I had heard about it at a seminar), I did research for a single niche on Google Trends and Google Adwords. I spent a day and a half conducting this research. When I conducted the same niche research with Niche Builder, I accomplished **more** in 30 minutes, and with **more accurate** information, than I had in that day and a half. This is because Niche Builder's results are so precise. You know exactly what your prospective niche is doing and whether this is a market to pursue.

So yes, there are free tools and they're good tools. But Niche Builder is just phenomenal. For the best possible success right out of the gate, I strongly encourage you to try Niche Builder today!

Now, back to what we do once you've figured out the niche and keyword phrases you want to market. You place them in order of the highest number of searches visitors to the lowest. You also take into consideration the ratio of competition compared to the number of visitors or searches. I advise this because, instead of having a keyword phrase that has 3,000 searches a month but 300,000 competition, I would prefer a keyword phrase that has 3,000 searches a month with only 5,000 other websites competing. That is the keyword you to focus on because it's more likely your target audience will find your website, and more likely your website will be ranked at the top of. So as you can see, determine which keyword phrases to use takes a little bit of strategy.

Once you have determined with keyword phrases will best reach your target audience, then pick 3 to 5 that you can research for your domain name — and the name of your website.

Now that you have identified a niche and its keywords, it's time to evaluate the potential of the product you have chosen to sell or promote.

IMPORTANT NOTE: Please understand that the numbers of "3,000" and "300,000" are a starting point. The important concept to remember is to make sure you have at least a couple thousand searches each month on a particular phrase. Any less and that keyword phrase is not being searched enough to make it worth your time, effort and money to pursue. In addition, keep the competition number to no more than 500,000. Always, less is best!

FIND SOURCES OF INCOME

So, there are tons of places where you can earn commissions off of products that you sell. I'm just going to touch on the most popular.

Amazon.com

The first one is Amazon.com
http://kippiperbooks.com/Amazon

It is free to join their Amazon Associates program. You simply go to their website, scroll to the bottom of the home page, and look for "Become an Affiliate" – as you can see circled in red in the next screenshot.

You click on that link, fill out the form, and you're ready to promote their products and receive commissions. You can earn up to 15% commission on everything that is purchased through your affiliate links. And I'm not talking about just books, videos and music; I'm talking about household appliances, clothing and furniture. Anything that Amazon sells you can earn a commission from if someone buys that product through your affiliate link. We'll go over affiliate links a little later.

Amazon Marketplace (the "Sell on Amazon" link right above the "Become an Affiliate" link) is another section in Amazon where you can sell your own items. For instance, if you knit baby afghans or if you have authored and printed your own books, you can sell them on Amazon marketplace

You can also resell items. For instance, say you bought a pair of jeans, tried them on and didn't like the style or they didn't fit, well, you can fold them up, put them back in the package, and resell them on Amazon Marketplace. You can effectively resell them in competition with Amazon or the department store that is selling through Amazon. This way you get some of your money back.

There are a lot of ways to take advantage of Amazon.

ClickBank

Another source of income is ClickBank
http://kippiperbooks.com/ClickBank

It is also free to join. ClickBank is an online digital warehouse, full of digital products: eBooks, training programs, software, games, designs. I mean designs anywhere from clothing designs, to house designs, to how to build a bird house, how to build a pool table – just about anything you can think of. Lots of self-help books, lots of tips and tricks books, online training programs, and services are sold through ClickBank.

Above is the screen shot of their home page. It is free to sign up. They have excellent training about how to sell products – both your own and as an affiliate of others' products. You can even buy products! I recommend you buy products through your own affiliate ID. That way you earn a commission on a product that you just bought – and in the end, you're not paying full price. ClickBank has great training, and they are fabulously dependable on payments.

You can earn up to 75% commissions or more. I say "more" because the standard commission range is around 50% to 75%. Some people offer their products on ClickBank at a 100% commission. The reason they do this is to get people in the "door" for their particular company. They give you the 100% commission for selling the product, and when a person purchases the product, they have that person's name, email address and contact information. They can make future income from this person by offering other products to them.

ClickBank is an excellent source of income, where you can search and find affiliate products that you promote on your website.

Digital Products You Have Purchased

Another great place to find products that you can promote are the products you purchase yourself – eBooks, training programs, software, services, games, designs — all those same things we talk about earlier.

Any product that you buy from a website, or any website where you shop, scroll down to the bottom of the website's home page. Look to see if they have an affiliate program or an associate program. And then sign up if it's a product that meets your niche!

BUILD YOUR BLOG WEBSITE

We have done our market research, and we have found products that we can sell. So now we build the niche website to market the products. Remember, without the market research and knowing that people are looking the niche that you are focusing on, and without knowing that you actually have products that you can offer, there is no point in spending the time building the blog website. But sine you've completed those steps, it's time to build your blog website.

Hosted vs. Self-Hosted Blogs

There are two different kinds of blog websites: one is "hosted and the other one is the "self-hosted".

The difference between the two is that "hosted" is considered a free website, and it's how I built the "house for sale" website. I chose the "hosted" kind of website because that was the first blog website I'd ever tried! I was kind of dipping my toes in at the time. A hosted website could be a Blogger website or Wordpress.com website.

A "self-hosted" website is one for which you buy the domain name, you have a hosting plan, and you use Wordpress.org as the platform for your website. We'll talk about the specifics of this little bit later.

The primary difference is "hosted" is free and "self-hosted" you have to pay a little.

Hosted Blogs

With hosted blog websites, the pros are that it is free and easy to use, but there are some pretty important cons. There are limitations in the kind of content you can put up, especially with Blogger, because they have censorship. They will check your blogs, and if they didn't like what they see, they can turn off your blog and shut down your whole website. Plus there are limitations on what you can advertise on your free blog website.

Also being free, they really don't have any obligation to you. I've known a number of people where their blogs disappear. In fact it was just few weeks ago that I saw on Facebook this person who I thought who had pretty much understanding of the industry and what she was doing with her business. She had a free blog website, and the company just totally shut down her blog! No notice! So years of work and effort and marketing she put into her website, gone in an instant. Hosted blog websites may be free and they may be easy to use, but is it worth the risk of losing all of what you've invested?

Self-Hosted

Next is self-hosted blog websites. The pros: you have control. You have control of the name of the domain. You have control over the software that you use as far as the features and the add-ons to website. You have control of what you advertise. You can put up any content that you want as long as it's legal.

I prefer and recommend Wordpress.org as the platform for your self-hosted blog website. Wordpress is the industry standard. It is the most used blogging platform out there. Plus it's easy to learn, easy to get help. There tons of forums on the Internet where you can post a question, ask "how do I do this?" and people come right out to the ready and let you know how to solve the problem you're having.

The cons of Wordpress.org and a self-hosted website: It does cost a little money, less than a hundred dollars per year. So it's not a lot! There's a little bigger learning curve. But again, there are lots of resources available to help you through this.

YOUR DOMAIN – YOUR COMPANY NAME

In building your website you've got to have a domain. A domain name is just like your company name.

Remember the keyword research we did earlier? The best keyword phrase with the best search results and most closely describes your niche, should be your domain name — which is equivalent of your company name on the Internet.

With the self hosted website, you own your domain. Owning a domain costs between $12-$15 per year. You should not be paying more than that. It's not necessary.

My number one place to go is GoDaddy.com
http://kippiperbooks.com/GoDaddy

There are lot of great domain registration and website hosting companies out there! I'm not disparaging any of them; my preference is GoDaddy, and there's a reason for this.

They have a great domain research tool, which most others do as well, but they have a great one. You research on the keyword you choose earlier to see if there is a domain that matches. You can register your domain right then in there. It is inexpensive.

GoDaddy has 24 hours a day, 365 days a year US-based customer support. This is huge! Because, it doesn't matter what time of the day or night you call them, they treat you with respect. And it doesn't matter how basic or how silly your question is, they will help you.

There are several important tips to remember when choosing your domain.

Remember to choose the keyword that you earlier put at the top of your list. You *always, always, always,* 99.99% all the time, **use a .com extension** to your domain. If you can't get a .com, then chose another keyword.

The only time you may not be using the .com is when you are a legitimate, recognized, non-profit organization. Then you can use .org.

Anything else really makes it difficult for people to find you on the Internet. Why?

People normally think of .com when they think of a website address. So if you just give them your address plus .com, it's easy for them to remember. If you give them your address plus .biz, or .info, or .me, or .us, then they have to remember that as well. And the chances of them remembering the correct extension is much, much less than if it was just .com. So keep it simple.

Use real words in your domain name. Don't use cutesy little funky spellings. Don't use numerals, unless it makes sense. If your company name is "123 Aluminum Siding", then yes, you'll want to use numerals in your domain for consistency in branding. But if you're creating something from scratch, keep it simple, use real words.

No hyphens in the domain name is another important thing. When you hyphenate your words in order to get a .com, Google does not recognize a hyphenated domain name as important as a domain name with no hyphens. In Google's hierarchy, a domain name with real words, no hyphen, and .com receives the highest authority ranking. You would have to work harder to get above those kinds of domains if you have a domain that has a different extension or has hyphens. That's a real important part of your strategy.

And of course again, match your domain name to your best keywords.

Hosting – Your Website's Office Space

For hosting, I'm going right back at the GoDaddy. Hosting is your websites' office space. It's where your website lives.

(Some people prefer to keep their website hosted with a different company than where their domain is registered. Their theory is, in case the hosting company develops an "attitude", they can always move their site to another hosting company and their site will not be offline for an extended period of time. For me, I've used GoDaddy since soon after they opened in 1997. I have NEVER experienced any sort of "attitude" or other issues with my websites. Obviously do what you prefer and what works best for your business.)

GoDaddy costs about $75 per year or less. It is worth going on to GoDaddy, and registering your domain is easy peasy. Just do it.

Avoid any upsell other than Economy website hosting with the Linux hosting platform. Linux is best for WordPress. Your alternative is Windows. I like Linux; I think it's more stable.

Also, if you have GoDaddy install your WordPress program, your hosting *may* cost more. You can manually install it yourself. So get a Plain Jane Economy Linux hosting plan, then call customer support and say "I want to manually install my WordPress, can you show me how?" They will walk you through every step. GoDaddy has just great customer service.

WordPress – Your Website's Interior Design

So now you have your domain, you have your hosting and your WordPress platform installed.

WordPress is a theme-based platform. Most templates are free. There are tons of themes that come with your WordPress. You could also go on the Internet and look for one that you can buy. But check out the free ones first because most of the time you're going to find what you're looking for.

Choose a theme that matches your niche. If you're selling a book on how to grow grass, you don't want teddy bears or hearts as your theme. It doesn't work, unless you are maybe selling pink grass.

One great thing about themes is that you can change them on the fly. This means, even when you have your website up and done, if you find another theme that you like even better, you just change it. All of your content stays there, nothing happens to it. But watch out for limitations on changing to a new theme because sometimes the extra feature settings, like plugins and widgets, may not be offered in the new theme. Or the new theme may need different sized graphics for the homepage, or other thinks. So just be careful when you're changing and make sure the new theme has everything you need.

DEVELOP CONTENT

The next thing to do is develop content for your blog, which means you have to write blog posts for you niche. Relax! The blog posts are important. They are the content of your site. They are the reason for people to come to your website is to read about the information provided.

There is a wide variety of blog posts topics that you could write and different kinds of articles, such as:

- You can write opinion article;
- You can write an article about your experience of something
- Or a story. People love stories because they can identify with them.
- You can research a topic and write an article about it.

Other ideas are:

Product Reviews

You can write a product review, which is perfect because you're reviewing the actual product that you're offering to sell. It doesn't matter whether it's a good product or a bad product, good review or bad review. Be honest because that's where your credibility is established with your readers. Even if it's a bad review, *always* link to the product with your affiliate ID, so you can earn a commission if someone decides to buy anyway.

Top Ten Tips or Things to Avoid

Great article fodder is the Top Ten List: top ten reasons to do something or top ten things to avoid. In fact, any "top" number works – top five, top 3, etc. People love "top" articles!

Guest Blogger

You can invite a guest blogger. Say you have your "growing grass" niche and your whole blog website is based on going grass, tips on going grass, species of grass, and things like that. What if you went to a guy who has a website on a special tool that aerates the ground so the water gets into the ground and keeps the roots healthy. You can ask him to write a guest blog about the benefits of ground aeration and the health of trees, grass and plants. What happens is you receive cross promotion to his audience (when he announced his guest blog to his readers) who now see your website, and your audience sees his website (because you give him author credit for the article and a link to his site) – and you both increase your viewer base.

Private Label Rights (PLR)

Another source is private label rights articles. PLR articles you pay for. They come as either individual articles or in a library of articles that you can reprint on your website, many times with the caveat that you give credit to the author. But there's another way of doing it.

You can also hire a writer or rewriter, because your blogs have to be original content. If you are going rewrite someone else's content, at least 30% of it needs to be original for it to be considered original content in the eyes of the search engines. They do check, and you can get penalized for having duplicate content. So this is very important.

There are great websites where you can hire writers.

Freelance.com
http://kippiperbooks.com/freelance

Odesk.com
http://kippiperbooks.com/oDesk

Fiverr.com
http://kippiperbooks.com/oDesk

I love Fiverr! You can buy just about anything on this website for $5, including hiring writers. One of the things I try to do is find writers that are US-based, because it is important to have a native, English-speaking writer. If you get someone who's not, there are going to be weird phrasings and grammar that you're going to have to spend your time to clean up – a waste of your time.

On Fiverr, there are gifts, graphics, video, social marketing, travel, and writing, advertising, music and video – so you can purchase all sorts of things. This is a fabulous service.

Keyword Rich

When you, or your hired writer, write your articles, the articles need to be keyword rich. Remember back when we were doing market analysis? The content of your website has to have those final keywords you chose.

For example, when you are working on the articles for, say, "growing Kentucky bluegrass" you should include that keyword phrase in your title, in your headlines and in your copy. *No more* than 7 total times, and they have to make grammatical sense. If your keyword phrase appears more than 7 times in your article, you can be penalized for spamming.

INCORPORATING INCOME LINKS

Next is incorporating your income links. The only recommended way is to use direct links to your products. Each product website – Amazon, ClickBank, any other sources – are going to have specific, easy-to-follow instructions on exactly how to code their links into your website. You determine the link format you wish to use and copy the code. Make sure your unique ID is included in the link because that's the *only* way you earn your commissions.

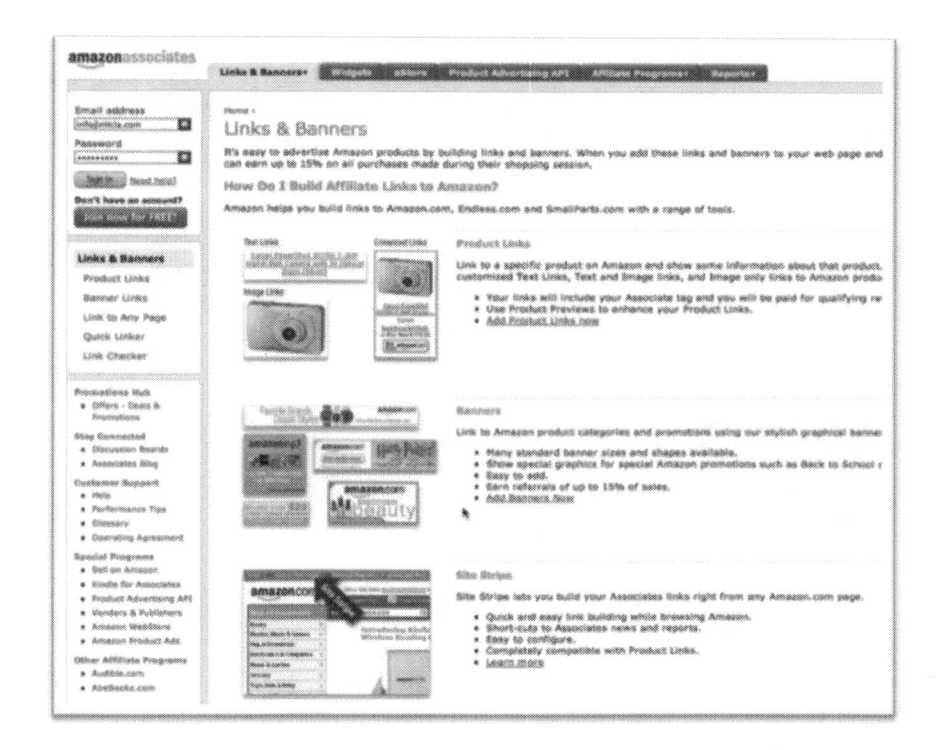

As you can see in the screenshot above, Amazon offers banner links, text links, and related links. Links and banners are links, and you can choose the formats you prefer. There are actual banners you can choose and Amazon designs it for you.

You also can use what they call "widgets". Widgets are little itty bitty search windows or product listing windows that Amazon automatically fills with products that are related to your niche. Or you can select other things, such as Amazon's daily deal. You also get to choose how big the windows are, and you get to choose where they appear on your website.

The big thing to remember is make sure you don't have too many of these ad windows. Depending on your niche, having a website full of all of these ads may make your site appear "busy". This can turn off your customer, make it difficult for them to read your articles, and leave them frustrated rather than buying.

Google Adsense also has a wonderful little link window that can be placed your website as well. With an Adsense window, you can earn commissions when people click on an ad in the window.

The best method, though, is direct links to the products in your articles. If you review a grass fertilizer, then you want to link specifically to the grass fertilizer product on the website that sells it. If you review lawn sprinklers, you want to link to the lawn sprinkler you recommend, or to each of the sprinklers in the whole group, if you wish.

ClickBank also has something similar called CBPress, and offers a little ClickBank window.

As you can see, there are lots of ways to earn affiliate commissions from products.

RANKING IN GOOGLE

Google loves blog websites!

Google considers blog websites as having the most up-to-date and relevant content. Most of the time Google is ranking a well-constructed blog website higher in the search rankings than a regular website with traditional SEO. Even if the blog website is only a couple of months old and the regular website is years old, Google ranks the blog websites higher. So this is a very powerful, folks.

And remember the keyword research earlier? It is important to use your keyword phrases when you're writing your blogs.

Also, there's the All-in-One SEO plugin. With this plugin, you can add your keywords to the underlying code of each page.

On your page and post titles, if it's appropriate, you need to use your keywords. If you're writing an article about Kentucky bluegrass, put "Kentucky bluegrass" in the title, and put it in your sub titles. Just make sure it makes content and grammatical sense! If it doesn't, then the search engines can penalize you.

It is strongly recommended that you organize your blog posts by different categories. You can use your keyword phrases for the names of the categories – once again, if it makes logical sense.

Each of your posts has the option to assign "tags". Tags are useful for a variety of reasons. Tags are another keyword source for search engines. Tags also allow your visitors to look at all articles under a particular tag. For instance, if you wrote an article about Kentucky bluegrass; and you have a tag of Kentucky bluegrass; and you've written two other articles also on Kentucky bluegrass, the visitor can click on the tag "Kentucky bluegrass" – because tags are hotlinks on your blog posts – and the visitor will be able to see all the articles about Kentucky bluegrass. So tags are a great cross-referencing tool – great for the visitor, very powerful for marketing and search engine placement.

How often should you post your blogs?

You need to post at least one blog per week, preferably two. The more blogs you post, and the better they are written, the faster your site will rank on the first page of Google.

A great easy way to write and post blogs is to schedule them. With Wordpress, you can postdate your blogs.

For example, let's say it's Sunday afternoon. You are sitting on your porch, watching the lawn sprinkler you recommended water the grass you told people how to grow, and you have some inspiration about lawn art or some other type of grass related or lawn related topics. You pull out your laptop; you write 3, 4, 5 blogs. Just boom! You're on a roll! You can take those blogs, put them into your website, and postdate the first one to appear on your site on Monday, and the second one to appear on your site on Thursday, then the others for sometime in the following week or even further into the future. Suddenly you have two or three weeks of writing done in one session. It's all posted. You don't have to worry about it!

That's why I say you can be a blogging affiliate marketer with just 2 to 5 hours a week. You can do this business on the schedule that meets your preference.

The important thing: *you have to be consistent.* That's how I was able to move the "house for sale" website so far up in the search engines – and *keep* it there. I posted at least two blogs per week. I was posting about flowers blooming, about the flowers, where the flowers were from, hummingbirds, birds, insects, features of the house – anything I could think about the house. I posted at least two blogs every single week for nine months. That's what makes blogging and affiliate marketing so powerful – and that's where people fail – being consistent. You've got to stay consistent.

"WASH, RINSE, REPEAT"

Now "Wash, Rinse, and Repeat". What do I mean?

Basically, you've got your blogging niche website for growing grass done, ok? And you've got your system of researching your products, posting your blogs, adding affiliate links, and you have income coming in!

Let's say you now want to create a blogging niche website about building birdhouses – because you like to build birdhouses.

Well! You just follow the system outlined in this book. You do market research, you find your niche, you find your products, you build your website, you write your blogs make sure they're keyword rich, you link to your affiliate products, and that website takes off!

The key to income on the Internet is multiple sources of income. So you need to have multiple websites out there!

I know that might seem little daunting, but trust me –when you get to the point where you have several websites out there, you'll be able to afford to hire someone to help you.

So that is basically how the whole system works!

Now you can see how powerful this system is for building a blog niche website, including affiliate marketing, and earning a steady income from the Internet when done right! Right?

It is very, very powerful, and it is simple to do. All it takes is for you to…

TAKE ACTION NOW!
****

I would like to say thank you for choosing my book since there are a large number of books on making money with blogging. If you liked my book, please, please take the time and leave a review – I would be extremely grateful.

One last thing. When you go to the last page of this book, Kindle will ask you to rate this book and share it with your friends on Facebook and Twitter. I would really appreciate it if you would share my book.

The very best of luck,

Kip Piper

ONE LAST THING…

As you can probably tell from my writing, my intention is to inspire and support more people to build a better financial future. It's a tough economy today, and I think personal growth in the field of small business is more important than ever before. Even though I have well over 20 years of experience as a successful small business owner and online entrepreneur, I don't have all the answers. In fact I'm still learning myself, I just have my own opinions, experiences and a passion for being my own boss to guide me through life.

Thank you for taking the time to read this book, I hope you enjoyed it. If you did I would really appreciate your support by taking the time to write a review for me on Amazon. Reviews really help the authors you enjoy to get noticed in a crowded marketplace, and it would allow me to continue writing the books for this series and other business books.   Please click below to let me know your thoughts:

http://kippiperbooks.com/UltimateGuide

All of my books are offered completely FREE on the launch and I want to reward loyal readers by offering my new books to them FREE of charge when they are released. So please visit my website www.KipPiperBooks.com and either download your free copy of *"28-Day Small Business Profit Plan: The Quick Start Guide to Business Success"* or just sign up to my newsletter in order to be kept informed when the next release is due. I hate spam, so I promise I won't send you any – not for love nor money!

Good luck! I wish you every success in your personal and business endeavors.

RESOURCES

Kip Piper Books
http://www.kippiperbooks.com

Kip Piper's Email
kip@kippiperbooks.com

"28-Day Small Business Profit Plan: The Quick Start Guide for Business Success"
http://www.kippiperbooks.com

San Angelo House for Sale
http://sanangelohouseforsale.Wordpress.com

Amazon.com
http://kippiperbooks.com/Amazon

ClickBank
http://kippiperbooks.com/ClickBank

Fiverr.com
http://kippiperbooks.com/oDesk

Freelance.com
http://kippiperbooks.com/freelance

GoDaddy.com
http://kippiperbooks.com/GoDaddy

Google Trends
http://www.google.com/trends/

Google Keyword Planner
https://adwords.google.com/ko/KeywordPlanner

Niche Builder
http://kippiperbooks.com/NicheBuilder

Odesk.com
http://kippiperbooks.com/oDesk

Ultimate Affiliate Marketing with Blogging Quick Start Guide
http://kippiperbooks.com/UltimateGuide

IN THEIR OWN WORDS

Genna Lepore
HubSpot Channel Account Manager

Kip Piper is insanely experience in the Internet marketing arena. Working with her is such a pleasure!

Frank Barnes

Kip is one of those rare individuals who has been working with the Internet since it hit the public in the 1990s. This has given her a unique understanding of the technology but more than that is her ability to distill the many technical aspects of website development, marketing, management and such down to a level that even the most novice "newbie" can understand. She has an incredible knack for translating the techno babble into everyday language. Anyone interested in starting an Internet business or wanting a refresher on the new ways of doing business on the Internet would be wise to listen to what Kip has to say.

Frank, a longtime follower of Kip's wisdom.

Deni Gainer

Thank you so much, Kip, for putting into plain English what so many instructors still manage to keep "secret" I their presentations. Now I certainly recognize scam offers and understand how the marketing works. I've done print/media marketing all of my life, NOW I feel confident in this arena as well.

A World Without MUSIC is NO World

My friend Kip is the "go to" person for the best step-by-step courses for starting an Internet business and making money with your online business.

Bethan Loves Kip Piper's Training!

Video – Go to the link below to watch Bethan's video testimonial.

http://kippiperbooks.com/bethan

ABOUT THE AUTHOR

KIP PIPER

http://twitter.com/kip_piper
http://facebook.com/TheRandomBlondeFanPage
http://linkedin.com/in/kippipertherandomblonde
http://www.kippiperbooks.com

Kip Piper and her company MTC Interactive graced the Austin Business Journal "Web Development and Marketing" top ten list from 1997-2004 (when she moved away from Austin).

Kip has also been featured in two articles appearing in Smart Computing magazine, including "Third Party Web Design".

Be sure to check out Amazon.com for Kip's Kindle eBooks.

MORE KINDLE BOOKS BY KIP PIPER

For all of my books, go to my website
http://www.kippiperbooks.com

MAKE MONEY ONLINE ENTREPRENEUR SERIES

http://www.kippiperbooks.com/makemoneyonlineseries

Now that you have finished the "Ultimate Affiliate Marketing With Blogging Quick Start Guide", you might be ready to really dive into creating and growing a successful and profitable online marketing business. If so, the "Make Money Online Entrepreneur Series" is for you!

The entire "Make Money Online Entrepreneur Series" consists of more than 20 books, specifically written as an entire online business success training course.

Beginning in August 2013, I released one book a week, in the proper order to ensure success. If you follow the series from Book 1 to the end, one week per book, you will complete a 5+ month training course and master being an online entrepreneur! Of course, you can finish the series faster. Just make sure you fully complete the lessons in each book before moving on to the next. This way your success will be greater!

This series is carefully designed to give you every building block you need to build a successful online business. All of the guesswork is taken away, and by following this series, you will avoid most of the common mistakes made by new and even experienced online entrepreneurs. All is revealed, nothing is left out!

The beauty of this series is that you can pick up any book on whatever topic you need at this moment. Or you can purchase each book as it is released. Or ultimately, yu can purchase the entire series in a bundle!

However you choose to use the information offered in this and the other books, you will be moving forward with intention and strategy for success in your business.

http://www.kippiperbooks.com/makemoneyonlineseries

The series includes these topics:
Book 1 – Freeing Up Your Time – VA's, Outsourcing & Goal Setting
Book 2 – Your Core Business, Niche & Competitors
Book 3 – Blogs & Emails: Your Link with Your Customers
Book 4 – Affiliate Marketing 101
Book 5 – Driving Traffic with Organic SEO
Book 6 – Power of Email Marketing
Book 7 – Quick Income Formula with Advanced Affiliate Marketing
Book 8 – List Building with Facebook
Book 9 – List Building with Twitter
Book 10 – List Building with LinkedIn
Book 11 – Compelling Opt-In Offers
Book 12 – Video Marketing
Book 13 – Paid Traffic with Facebook Ads
Book 14 – Web Analytics
Book 15 – Product Creation – Research
Book 16 – Product Creation – Creation
Book 17 – Product Creation – Tie In
Book 18 – Product Creation – Promotion
Book 19 – Presentation Based Selling 1
Book 20 – Presentation Based Selling 2
Book 21 – Presentation Based Selling 3
Book 22 – Writing Great Sales Letters
Book 23 – List Building with Joint Ventures

http://www.kippiperbooks.com/makemoneyonlineseries

Made in United States
Orlando, FL
02 July 2024